Contributors

D.C.Gomez
Dennis Barger
Diane Green
Ellen Wood
Johan Ingler
J.L.Yarrow
Suzy Vadori
Stephen Weinstock
Angela Van Breemen
Michelle Owusu
J.R.Lightfoot
Candace Macphie
Don Sawyer
Dr. Katherine Hutchinson-Hayes
Edward Willett
Kay Sparling
CJ Wheeler
Robert Germaux

Review Tales
A Book Magazine For Indie Authors

Founder & Editor in Chief: S. Jeyran Main
Publisher: Review Tales Publishing & Editing Services
Print & Distribution: Ingram Spark
Designs: Pexels
ISBN 978-1-988680-72-9 (Paperback)
ISBN 978-1-988680-73-6 (Digital)
www.jeyranmain.com
For all inquiries, please contact us directly.

Photo Credits from Pexels:
Pexel-1480914-2852438
Pexel-alinevianafoto-2465877

A BOOK MAGAZINE FOR INDIE AUTHORS

REVIEW TALES

Editor's Note

Dear Readers,

Can you believe we've reached Issue #15? What an incredible journey it's been! As we welcome the warmth and wonder of summer, I'm filled with gratitude and joy to present to you this very special Summer Edition of the Review Tales Book Article Magazine.

This issue is especially dear to our hearts — not just because of the sunshine and longer days, but because of the rich content that fills these pages. It's packed with meaning, emotion, and insight. You'll find powerful confessions, deep reflections, and thought-provoking articles that speak directly to the soul. We've also included a selection of Editor's Picks — a handful of books that have inspired, challenged, and refreshed us in all the best ways. Whether you're in need of encouragement, looking for a new perspective, or just hoping to unwind with a good read, there's something here for you.

This issue wouldn't be what it is without the incredible individuals who lent their voices, thoughts, and hearts to it. To all our contributors: thank you. Your honesty, your vulnerability, and your passion are woven into every article, and we are honored to share your words with our readers. You've helped create a space that's not only thought-provoking but deeply human.

To our faithful readers and supporters — whether you've been with us from the very beginning or are just discovering us now — thank you from the bottom of our hearts. Your support, encouragement, and enthusiasm fuel this magazine's mission and spirit. You remind us that storytelling still matters, that truth has power, and that words can still light the way.

As always, our goal is simple: to provide content that nourishes your mind, softens your heart, and draws you closer to wisdom, purpose, and truth. And what better time than summer to do just that? So pour yourself something cool, find a cozy spot under the sun or shade, and settle in. From all of us here at the Review Tales Book Article Magazine — enjoy the read, enjoy the warmth, and enjoy the season.

With gratitude and sunshine,

Jeyran Main

Editor-in-Chief
Review Tales Magazine

SUMMER 2025 | ISSUE 15

Contents

Finding Our Purpose in Turbulent Times
D.C. Gomez

Elizabeth Gilbert said in her book Big Magic that, as authors, we create "brain-candy." Like most candy, art might not technically be a necessity. But during difficult times, it can be the anchor we need to weather the storm. Books, specifically, have a way of uniting people and helping us escape our current situations and problems. During these difficult times in our history, books are in greater demand.

This idea of helping people disconnect from their everyday stress and escape into a magical world inspired a crazy and wild idea for me. What could I add to this narrative that is taking shape around us? How could I be of service? Those questions plagued me for months. Then, in the middle of an author's mastermind, it all clicked: I can share my words with the world at no cost to anyone.

The more I let the idea play around in my head, the more it resonated with me. If I could add one thing to this narrative, I could give joy, no questions asked, no commitment from the reader, besides one book they would enjoy. That is how the idea to give away a million eBooks of Death's Intern and spread joy started.

But how was I going to pull this off? Let's be honest, I'm still a small indie author writing Urban Fantasy. Where do I even start this plan? The details threatened to overwhelm me. Fear and doubt kept trying to take over. What were people going to say? This would end badly if I failed. What if I made a fool of myself and aimed too big?

It is easy to give in to self-doubt and indecision. The impostor syndrome monster can easily derail us by filling us with fears. I reminded myself that there is no way I can fail, because every book I give away is one more smile I have helped bring to this world. With a newfound joy, I'm ready to find creative ways to spread more joy.

Happy Reading, my friend!

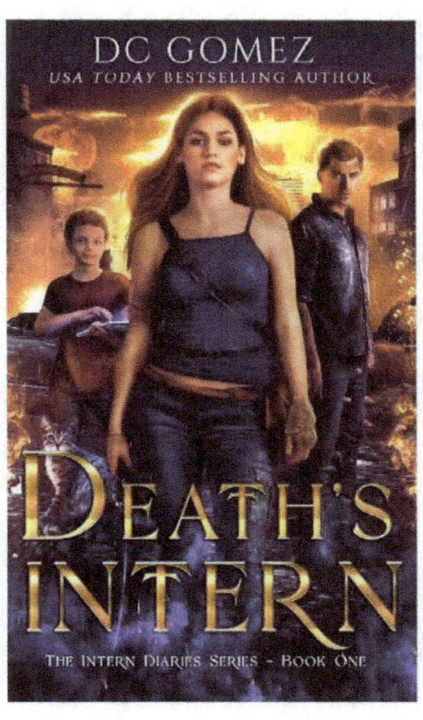

A Second Career
Dennis Barger

Planning for retirement from a successful 44-year career in the insurance industry, I was advised to find three to four things I would do to stay busy. One of my listed items was to write a novel. I graduated from the University of Cincinnati with a BA in English Literature and a Business Certificate. Additionally, my maternal grandfather, a high school English teacher, had always given us books at Christmas. This spurred my desire to write a book.

Several ideas were developed, but nothing seemed to resonate until I remembered a story I heard while vacationing as a young boy on the Outer Banks, NC, about German U-boat sailors occupying the cottages during the closed winter months. I embarked on researching this and other similar events. I spent over a year researching historical events, people, and facts, providing accuracy to the fictional adventure of my main characters. An extensive bibliography is provided to help the reader separate fact from fiction.

A Secret Soldier's Confession is a fictional story set in the present using historical events. I created an action-adventure tale to keep the reader entertained. The story features a female protagonist, an international setting, a historical hook, and puzzle-solving escapades. The adventure includes an abundance of location details, so the reader feels immersed in the journey.

After a year of research, I wrote the novel during the second year, fine-tuning it through beta readers and completing the initial manuscript. I received advice from fellow author Dana Alioto, Hey Nineteen: A Memoir of Growing up in Milwaukee, Wisconsin. In addition to beta reading, Dana provided insights into the publishing process, especially the challenges of finding a publisher.

I queried numerous literary agents, who all declined to represent my book. I did not expect the amount of work necessary to find literary agents. This included finding lists of agents, researching each agent's submission requirements, and tailoring a specific query letter. The process demanded a work effort comparable to the book research. I eventually found W. H. Wax Publishing, LLC, a southwest regional publisher. The publisher designed the book cover, delivered expert editing, and launched worldwide distribution.

Finding the publisher occurred through a fortuitous event. My wife and I were vacationing in Italy, and I met Jason Horn, author of Crossing Paths, on a train. The conversation sparked Jason's introduction to his publisher, W. H. Wax Publishing, LLC.

I intend to start an outline for a second novel. And I continue to work on my retirement list, along with keeping focus on faith, family, and friends.

The Power and Popularity of Short Stories: A Tale of Discovery in Dinosaur Land

Diane Green

In today's fast-paced world, where the acronym "TLDR" ("too long; didn't read") defines how many people consume content, short stories are experiencing a well-deserved renaissance. Their brevity makes them an ideal fit for modern lifestyles—perfect for busy professionals, parents juggling responsibilities, or anyone craving a meaningful escape without the commitment of a full-length novel. The impact of short fiction is undeniable, offering depth and resonance in a concise format.

But some stories hold more than just brevity—they hold secrets.

At first glance, Dinosaur Land is a 59-page tale about a 12-year-old foster child, Tommy, whose street smarts have made him wary of trust, love, and second chances. Sent to live with an old man he mockingly calls "Grandpa," Tommy expects disappointment. But something about this new home unsettles him—not in fear, but in curiosity. Grandpa doesn't push, doesn't pry, yet seems to understand Tommy in a way no one else has.

And then there are the dinosaurs.

Scattered across the property stand towering relics of a forgotten roadside attraction, weathered by time and mystery. Grandpa speaks of them with reverence, as if they are more than just decaying structures. He is a man of deep faith, but also of quiet conviction—holding knowledge that may be more than Tommy is ready to grasp.

As the story unfolds, Tommy begins to wonder: Is there more to Grandpa than meets the eye? What is it about these lifelike figures that makes them feel as if they are waiting? When Grandpa speaks in parables and scripture, is he revealing wisdom... or a warning?

Like Alice Munro's Nobel Prize-winning short fiction, Dinosaur Land proves that powerful storytelling does not require excessive length to leave a lasting impact. Some discoveries come quickly. Others take a lifetime to understand.

What Tommy finds in Dinosaur Land may not be what he expected—but once a secret is unearthed, it can never be buried again.

Want to Grow Younger?

Ellen Wood

Fifteen years ago, Harvard-affiliated researchers published remarkable findings: gene therapy reversed aging in mice. Age-related decline — including reduced brain function, failing organs, and graying fur — was not only slowed but reversed. The mice literally grew younger. Dr. Ronald DiPinho, a geneticist at Dana-Farber and Harvard Medical School, said the study revealed a core pathway behind aging, suggesting immense promise.

The researchers boosted telomerase, an enzyme that lengthens telomeres, and watched signs of aging disappear. Brain function returned to normal, organs revived, and fur darkened. The implications are staggering: Could humans experience the same reversal?

Fast forward to July 12, 2023. Scientists from Harvard Medical School, the University of Maine, and MIT published another breakthrough titled "Chemically Induced Reprogramming to Reverse Cellular Aging." Lead researcher Dr. David Sinclair shared, "Until recently, the best we could do was slow aging. New discoveries suggest we can now reverse it." According to Sinclair, the findings could lead to a single pill capable of improving eyesight and treating age-related diseases — a Nobel Prize–worthy achievement.

While the science advances, we shouldn't sit back. There are steps you can take now to grow younger. Alzheimer's Disease, for instance, is fatal and disproportionately affects women; two-thirds of patients and caretakers are women. If you're looking for scientific proof that age reversal is possible, the evidence is here.

In my two-volume book, The Secret Method for Growing Younger — endorsed by Marianne Williamson and five M.D.s, including anti-aging expert Dr. Terry Grossman — I share actionable strategies. Dr. Grossman and I even gave speeches together. I carry the APO-e4 gene, which increases Alzheimer's risk. My mother died of the disease. Yet, I reversed my early symptoms — memory lapses, trouble finding words, and reliance on sticky notes — and regained mental clarity.

I continue these practices daily. My upcoming book, The Five Tibetan Rites – the Right Way, coming in 2025, reveals physical movements that support youthfulness. Until then, search "Five Tibetan Rites – Ellen Wood" on YouTube to follow along.

Now, at 88, I have sharp memory, strong health, vibrant creativity, and no gray hair. Visit www.howtogrowyounger.com to learn more.

EVERY ENDING IS A NEW BEGINNING

Johan Ingler

Anyone who's tried to make a career out of writing knows about rejection. It's not fun, but I believe it's a healthy part of the process. There's no harm in realizing you need to work a little harder. I've received my fair share of refusals, and while none have ever brought a smile to my face, they've consistently helped motivate me. I've always thought that if I believe in something with every ounce of my being, there must be someone else out there who gets it, too. Right?

I've long aspired to be a novelist, but I chose to study screenwriting to learn the ins and outs of story-building. I figured the lessons would be applicable to any type of writing. Before the first semester was over, I had written the first draft of Frankie & Chair, not waiting to learn if I was even doing it "correctly." I must have done something right, because I won a couple of awards for it and was on my way to turning it into a movie. I felt like I was living the dream.

But then reality did its thing and handed me a heap of choices too big to handle. Before I knew it, I was standing by the side of the road with nothing but a worn-out suitcase full of hard-earned life lessons. Along the way, I had grown to love Frankie & Chair more than any other story I'd written. It had been my friend through thick and thin, and even though I was out of ideas for getting it onto the screen, I couldn't let it wither away. So, I turned it into a novel.

The submissions began, the rejections started coming back—and I realized I had to find another way. Like I said, if I believe in something with every part of me... And here we are, almost ten years since that first draft. My beloved Frankie & Chair is finally out in the world, independently published. Whatever comes of this, nothing will ever truly be the end—only the next beginning.

YOU JUST FINISHED YOUR NOVEL...
YOU NEED A MANUSCRIPT
OVERVIEW!

J.L. Yarrow

As an author, you've poured your heart and soul into your novel—congratulations! Now what? Should you find an agent, submit to publishers, or try self-publishing? While there are many options, my advice is: don't rush.

Sending your manuscript to a hundred agents might feel productive, but if it's not ready, that could mean a hundred rejections. You may believe your novel is brilliant and destined to sell itself—and maybe it is—but success without preparation is extremely rare. Most writers need to hone more than just their manuscript; they develop query letters, synopses, loglines, and attend conferences to pitch to agents and editors. And even then, only the strongest submissions get noticed.

Let's say your first chapter and synopsis catch an agent's eye—great! But how polished is the rest of your novel? Major publishers and agents often require additional editing steps before considering representation. One essential step is a Manuscript Overview (MOV), also known as developmental editing.

You might think your story is solid. Maybe your friends loved it, or it's even won awards. But if you've received multiple rejections, it's worth considering an MOV. I say this from experience. My novel won three literary awards, yet both an agent and two publishers told me to get a developmental edit. At first, I resisted—why should an award-winning author need more edits?

But I went through with it (I co-write with my wife), and we're so glad we did. An MOV was like a college course tailored to our story. We refined our writing, tightened the plot, expanded world-building, and cut down from 585 pages to 440. We trimmed repetition and made sure every word advanced the narrative. Afterward, we received much more interest and went on to publish two novels.

Getting a Manuscript Overview was the best investment we made in our writing journey. If you're serious about publishing and want your novel to stand out, don't skip this step. It could be the key to moving from promising manuscript to published book.

I DIDN'T KNOW WRITING COULD BE A JOB—UNTIL IT BECAME MINE

Suzy Vadori

I always knew I would write a book one day, but nobody ever told me that writing could be a job. So, I worked as a business executive, building other people's dreams for the first 20 years of my career. Then, while on maternity leave with my third child (she's 13 now), I finally sat down and started a draft of my first novel. Writing a full-length book was much harder than I'd thought it would be. I was great at spelling and grammar, but there was so much more to it.

I got to work, studying with every editor, agent, and publisher I met at conferences and online. Four and a half years later, I'd figured out a replicable writing process and turned that book idea into my debut novel, The Fountain, which went on to sell thousands of copies and win awards. By that time, I'd gone back to work and was busy juggling business travel and my young family while finishing my Young Adult Fantasy series. But I still didn't believe that writing could be my job.

By the time Book 2 in the series was released, I was being asked to speak and teach about writing, and to help other writers get their books ready for publishing. I'd learned a ton on my journey and was teaching my replicable process to other writers by breaking down many of the complex writing concepts I'd studied into manageable steps they could use to get their amazing ideas onto the page in book form.

Writers I worked with were seeing huge progress with their writing and asking for more and more of my time—until I didn't have time to work at my day job anymore. Doing all things writing had somehow become my job when I wasn't looking.

I've since worked with thousands of writers as an editor and book coach to get the books they always dreamed of writing written and shared with readers. It's been the most challenging and rewarding job I've ever had, and I'll never look back.

THE QARAQ
Stephen Weinstock

My writing career began while I was still a musician—improvising at the piano for modern dance classes at The Fame School in NYC and crafting scores for choreographers. I carved out writing time by squeezing it into the margins of my collaborative life. Then I retired, moved to the peace of upstate New York, and prepared to settle into a blissful fantasy writer's existence.

But I faced a dilemma that plagues every writer: solitude. At times, it's luscious. But I was used to high-charged teenagers, inspiring collaborators, and a balance between human contact and creative time. I needed a new equilibrium. To counter the isolation, I walked the dog, saw neighbors, and called friends—but none of those interactions engaged my writer self.

Then I discovered what so many writers rely on: the Writer Get-Together. These meet-ups come in many forms and are readily available both in person and online. There's a critique group at my local library. There are online groups where you write your own work simultaneously with others (like "Shut Up and Write"). There are workshops where a facilitator assigns prompts.

I started my own local Accountability Group. We meet every two weeks, having set personal writing and marketing goals at the previous meeting. As we share the outcomes of our goals, rich topics often arise for discussion: self-publishing, character arcs, research resources, and more. The group has strengthened everyone's writing practice.

Another favorite social writing experience is the writer's retreat. I attended one in the blustery weather outside Ottawa, Canada, this January (was I crazy?). I expected to get a lot of writing done and learn from the coaches—but the greatest benefit was being around a diverse group of writers. The camaraderie surrounding our universal struggles and joys was unforgettable.

Writer's conferences in your genre. Coffee with a fellow poet. Surrendering your draft to a trusted editor. Contributing to a literary journal! All these variations make beautiful music on the theme of social connection for writers. I highly recommend this meaningful shift from the lonely craft. Enjoy your solitude—then dash it!

to be a Fae by Tricia Copeland

When did you first realize you wanted to be a writer?

I first realized I wanted to be a writer after completing the manuscript for my first two books and receiving excited feedback from friends and family. Their love for my story and encouragement to continue the series and develop the characters made me feel validated and reinforced my passion for writing and storytelling. While I always loved writing, having others appreciate my work gave me a real boost.

How do you schedule your life when you're writing?

When I'm working on a book, I like to write every day. Writing daily keeps the story moving, and the characters and plot fresh in my mind. Throughout the day, even while doing chores or running errands, I'm constantly thinking about what I just wrote—whether it fits the characters, what their next challenges might be, and where the story is heading. For months, my characters and storyline take up most of my mental space.

What would you say is your interesting writing quirk?

My most interesting writing quirk is that I never imagined myself as a writer. Unlike many authors who say they wrote from a young age, I actually hated writing until graduate school. As a science major, writing never clicked for me—until my graduate professor helped me write my first scientific article. Somehow, that made sense, and I developed a love for technical writing. From there, my passion for creative writing grew.

Where did you get your information or idea for your book?

The idea for the Realm Chronicles series came from an image of a fairy crouched between grasses in a meadow—apprehensive, guarded, yet determined. This image inspired me to write a story for an anthology about fantasy creatures with mental health challenges. That fairy became Princess Titania, the protagonist of my series. She's the only surviving child of her royal line, trained to rule, but at fifteen, her anxiety and panic attacks make her question her ability to be queen.

A Black Woman's Pain by Michelle Owusu-Hemeng

When did you first realize you wanted to be a writer?

I've always loved storytelling, but I think I truly realized I wanted to be a writer when I was a teenager. I would write little scenes in my head to process life, and I was obsessed with sci-fi and fantasy. It wasn't just about escaping; it was about creating whole new worlds where anything felt possible. That spark never left.

What would you say is your interesting writing quirk?

I write out loud. I speak my character's lines and even move like them. It's very much actor-meets-writer. I also imagine camera angles in every scene, probably thanks to my filmmaking background.

How did you get your book published?

I'm currently in the querying phase. I've finished writing my middle-grade sci-fi/fantasy novel *Plant Blood* and am actively pitching it to agents. I've learned so much about the publishing process, especially the importance of patience and perseverance.

Where did you get your information or idea for your book?

Plant Blood came from my love of nature, futurism, and the question of how young girls can be powerful changemakers. Climate change, AI, and spiritual magic all came together in this wild world I couldn't stop thinking about.

What was one of the most surprising things you learned in creating your book?

That rewriting is an act of self-trust. I threw out my first draft entirely and started from scratch. It was terrifying, but it made the story so much better. It reminded me that I grow as a writer by listening to my gut.

Retribution: Chronicles of Reaper Book II by J.R. Lightfoot

When did you first realize you wanted to be a writer?

I don't know if there was such a moment. I started writing as a way to handle stress at work. Writing/reading is an escape for me that I really enjoy.

How do you schedule your life when you're writing?

I will attack the computer once I have spent time with my family. Then I find a quiet spot in the house and the magic begins.

What would you say is your interesting writing quirk?

Sarcasm. I am a very sarcastic person and I take every opportunity to include it whenever possible. I've found that my sarcasm breaks up serious moments in the story and gets the reader to giggle a bit.

How did you get your book published?

I self-publish. With my first book, I tried traditional queries. After the first million "I am sure someone will pick you up, just not us," I prayed and decided these were my stories, and that is what is most important

Where did you get your information or idea for your book?

As a teacher in an inner-city school, I often asked my students why they don't read. "They don't look like us." So I wanted to create a Conan the Barbarian type hero who was Black. It has worked, as several students have bought and read my books. Some continue to search for books with heroes that look like them.

What do you like to do when you're not writing?

Play, coach, and referee soccer. Play with my granddaughter and train my kids to reach and achieve their goals.

What was one of the most surprising things you learned in creating your book?

I learned I love to write action and battles but have to force myself during the plot and setup moments of the book. I don't feel comfortable writing romance, and I don't know why.

Is there anything you would like to confess about as an author?

After I write my book, I read it for grammar errors, then I read it for flow, then I read it for enjoyment. Then I publish it. I am a teacher; I have no budget.

Life Strikes Back by Candace Macphie

Where did you get your information or idea for your book?

My five-part Back in a Year series is based on my hilarious and messy around-the-world backpacking adventures in the '90s. Not only do you get to travel the world, but you also experience life before cell phones and having the internet at your fingertips. It's a wild ride filled with laughter, cringy, scary, and happy moments. But best of all, it's an easy read to kick back with.

What would you say is your interesting writing quirk?

I listen as much as I read my writing. When I get into a scene, I write it, then review. The most important part of my review is listening to the scene. I use the Read Aloud function on Word, and it helps me catch any missed words or places that need to be smoothed out.

What do you like to do when you're not writing?

Out late, every night, rock and roll... Nah. I've had four surgeries in the last five years. Two of them were labral tear repairs on either hip. The recovery for this can be up to a year. And it's not super fun. So I've taken up aquafit. Yup. I said it. Aqua aerobics. And it's helped my recovery immensely. My sixty- to eighty-year-old friends and I meet three times a week and groove to the oldies in the pool. If I'm not at the pool, I'm spending time with my kids and creating new cake creations. The last one, blueberry crumble cake, was a big hit. The only snag is that I never write recipes down, so each version is always slightly different.

What was one of the most surprising things you learned in creating your book?

Writing is creative and fun. Editing is an exercise in meticulous patience and perseverance. Both of these tasks are very different and require very different strengths. So I had to hone both of them to create a good book that the reader will enjoy. Not only does the story need to be compelling, but I also need to put my time into editing to ensure it's a smooth and non-repetitive reading experience.

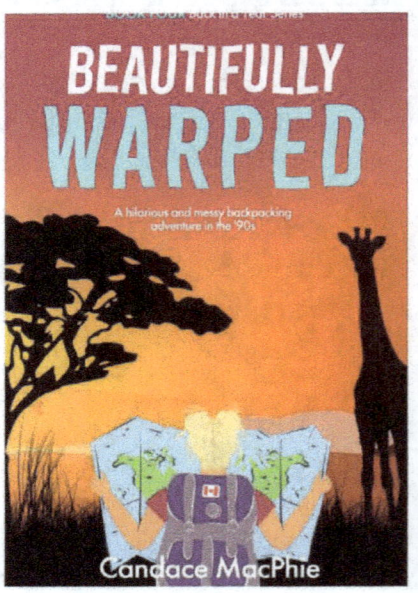

The Tunnels of Buda by Don Sawyer

How do you schedule your life when you're writing?

Generally speaking, not very well. Before I retired, my writing schedule (such as it was) was pretty well determined by life. When I was working as an educator, including long periods overseas in West Africa, I wrote when I could. I have two wonderful daughters, and when they were young, I'd get them to bed, tell them a bedtime story (the origin of the Miss Flint books, including The Meanest Teacher in the World), draw them a lunch bag joke (later collected in The Lunch Bag Chronicles), and then grab an hour or two of writing before crashing. A lot of my writing took place between 10:00 pm and 1:00 am.

Now that I have more time, I try to get as much writing in as I can before 1:00 pm. After that, things just seem to get entirely out of hand. But safe to say, I am not the highly disciplined, write-three-pages-a-day, take-one-hour-off-for-lunch-and-get-back-to-work author that I admire. (Theoretically, I think all those adjectives should be connected with hyphens.)

What was one of the most surprising things you learned in creating your book?

That there really is an abandoned subway system under New York called the Beach Pneumatic Transit system. It opened in 1870, was abandoned a few years later, and largely forgotten. While I exaggerated the extent of that ancient line as well as the size of the station, I was amazed that such remarkable innovation and construction could be utterly forgotten. It was a perfect home for my world of forgotten knowledge, misfit geniuses, and a refuge for practitioners of ancient arts and holders of lost knowledge.

Is there anything you would like to confess about as an author?

The editor-writer relationship can be tense. After struggling with two editors—one due to my inexperience with the editorial process, the other for trying to sanitize my work—I spoke with a seasoned writer friend. He explained editors tend to make changes in three ways: helpful edits you welcome, unnecessary ones you tolerate, and damaging ones you fight.

When a new editor was assigned to my latest book, I preemptively outlined those categories in my reply, hoping to set expectations. A few days later, he responded firmly: "We can do this cooperatively or adversarially. Your choice."

Not the smoothest start. I apologized, and we got to work. Though we disagreed on one major point, we worked through it—and nearly all his suggestions ultimately improved the book.

A Fifth of the Story by Dr. Katherine Hutchinson-Hayes

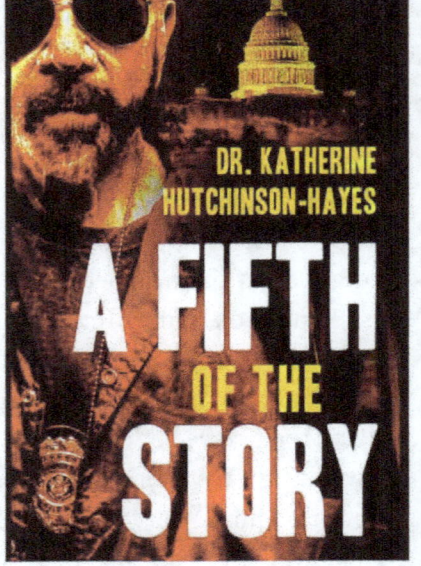

When did you first realize you wanted to be a writer?

From a young age, inspired by my father's captivating storytelling, I was enchanted by the power of words. His tales sparked my imagination, and I knew I wanted to share my own stories with the world.

How do you schedule your life when you're writing?

I create a detailed writing schedule for my blog a year in advance, which helps me stay organized and focused. Working alongside nine other writers, I structure my days with specific writing blocks and set weekly, monthly, and yearly goals to maintain productivity and foster collaboration.

What would you say is your interesting writing quirk?

I love setting the mood with candles and jazz piano, sipping homemade lattes or herbal tea to create a cozy atmosphere that inspires creativity and helps me focus.

How did you get your book published?

I've self-published three nonfiction books supporting nonprofits I care about and transitioned into fiction through networking. A former boss shared my thriller proposal with a publisher, leading to my first traditional publishing experience.

Where did you get your information or idea for your book?

I draw heavily from real events and my husband's military intelligence experience, investing significant time in research to ensure my thrillers are authentic and immersive.

What do you like to do when you're not writing?

I'm passionate about fitness—martial arts, swimming, running, biking—and I volunteer as an online art teacher for Guatemalan students through Light for the Future. My family and I also love traveling to explore new cultures.

What was one of the most surprising things you learned in creating your book?

Writing deepened my understanding of my characters and myself. The characters reflected aspects of my life and relationships, which enriched my storytelling and strengthened my bond with my husband, who helped shape their authenticity.

Fireboy by Edward Willett

When did you first realize you wanted to be a writer?

Pretty early on. I was a voracious reader, which naturally led me to want to write my own stories. I wrote my first complete short story, Kastra Glazz: Hypership Test Pilot, when I was eleven. Encouragement and feedback from my English teachers helped me write three novels during high school. Though I was interested in many things—music, art, theatre, science—by the time I headed to university, I had already decided to pursue writing.

How did you get your book published?

Fireboy is actually over my sixtieth published book, fiction and nonfiction combined—I've lost count! It's my first novel in almost two years. I've been published by many different houses, from small to large; DAW Books in New York, a major sci-fi/fantasy publisher, has published twelve of my novels. Each book's publishing journey is unique.

For Fireboy, I submitted it to a publisher who expressed interest but then took so long to respond that during the wait, I built Shadowpaw Press into a notable Canadian traditional publisher. So, I pulled Fireboy from the original publisher and am releasing it through Shadowpaw Press this year, along with eight other books by various authors.

It's only the second original novel of mine published by Shadowpaw, and it's been rewarding to apply what I've learned about publishing to my own work.

Where did you get your information or idea for your book?

The inspiration came from a single striking image: "I knew things were getting weird when I saw my best friend's face in the campfire." From that haunting image of a boy's face in the flames, I built the story, setting, and characters. That image was the seed from which the entire tale grew.

What do you like to do when you're not writing?

Music is a big part of my life outside writing. I sing with a talented self-directed choir called Wascana Voices, which rehearses weekly and performs two concerts a year. I also occasionally perform in musical theatre; last year, I played Maurice in a community production of Disney's Beauty and the Beast. I'm a member of Canadian Actors' Equity and have done some professional theatre over the years.

When I'm not writing or performing, I'm often managing the details of running my one-man (plus a cat) traditional publishing company.

Mission Thaw by Kay Sparling

How do you schedule your life when you're writing?

I turn off all communication devices and head to my office just as others are turning in for the night. I burn the midnight oil in the quiet —many times finishing my work as the sun rises. Occasionally, I escape to an isolated cabin in the northern woods to live out the author dream for a few days, completely immersed in writing.

What would you say is your interesting writing quirk?

I wrote a lot of funny comeback lines for my protagonist, Kaitlyn Stewart. Usually, these sassy remarks come out in very dangerous or serious moments, when everyone else on the team turns grim and quiet. Kaitlyn's witty sense of humor is her way of keeping morale up, even in the darkest situations.

Where did you get your information or idea for your book?

Initially, much of it came from my own eyewitness experiences during the years the mission takes place. Later, I supplemented that with research—diving into media reports, history books, and interviewing intelligence agents, refugee victims, and their families.

As a child, what did you want to do when you grew up?

When I was five, I saw The Sound of Music at the movie theatre. During intermission, I declared to my entire extended family that I was going to do THAT! When my mother asked what THAT was, I said, "I'm going to be in The Sound of Music." Two years later, at age seven, I was singing the role of Gretl, and I never looked back. For as long as I can remember, I've wanted to sing and act on stage.

How do you process and deal with negative book reviews?

As I write this, I haven't received any negative book reviews—knock on wood—but I know they're coming. I plan to handle them as I did in my long singing career: read them, see if there's anything I can learn or take away, and if not, just remind myself, "That's their point of view," and carry on. I'm also reminded of something my opera agent once told me. He asked, "Kay, as you perform in Europe, how many statues and tombs have you seen commemorating composers, musicians, playwrights, and conductors?" I said, "A lot." He nodded knowingly. It put things in perspective for me.

HARVESTING EVIL BY CJ WHEELER

On the idyllic shores of Lake Michigan, the quiet resort town of Port Orion, Michigan has become prime hunting ground for a serial killer.

One by one, young, beautiful women's corpses continue to surface, while the timeline between each victim is shrinking.

As Sheriff Parker Anderson pulls her inexperienced team together to find the madman terrorizing her community, a third victim surfaces, and the Port Orion Sheriff's department finds its resources stretched to the limit. As pressure mounts, Parker reaches out to the FBI for assistance.

Enter Special Agent Oliver Locke, who has seen more than his fair share of serial homicide cases, though even he has not encountered a psychopath with this level of violence. Working a serial case against a cunning criminal mind who leaves no evidence, will test his expertise and determination.

As the window of opportunity to prevent another victim closes, Sheriff Anderson and Agent Locke will need to set aside their personal differences to catch this maniac.

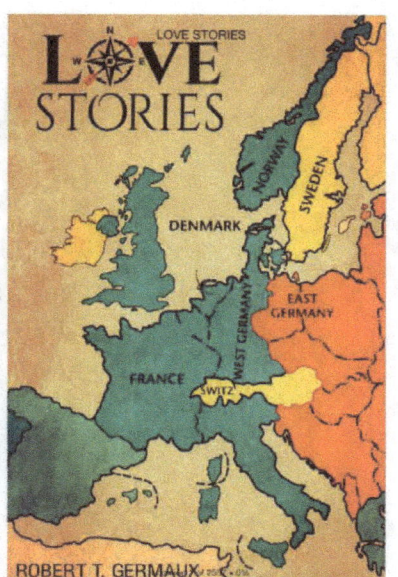

LOVE STORIES BY ROBERT GERMAUX

In 1966, seventeen-year-old Cindy attended a youth conference in Norway, unknowingly capturing the heart of Dean, a fellow traveler. Though he never confessed his love, decades later, a lost letter and poem from the day before Cindy's wedding in 1969 revealed his deep feelings. Married to the author for over 50 years, Cindy rediscovered her travel journal and memories of that summer, inspiring a semi-biographical novel, Love Stories. The book shifts between 1966 and 1989, imagining Dean's return. Ultimately, it's not just about Dean's love, but the enduring relationship between the author and the love of his life—Cindy.